Also By Matthew Barnes

1. **Ancient Egyptian Enlightenment Series:**
   (amazon.com/author/matthewbarnes)
   The Emerald Tablet 101
   The Hermetica 101
   The Kybalion 101
2. **The Zen-nish Series:** (amazon.com/author/matthewbarnes)
   The Tao Te Ching 101
   Albert Einstein, Zen Master
   The Tao Te Ching 201
   Jesus Christ, Zen Master
   Dr. Seuss, Zen Master
3. **The Hindu Enlightenment Series:**
   The Bhagavad Gita 101
4. **Investing Series (Zen-vesting)**
   (amazon.com/author/matthewbarnes)
   Investing 101
   Investing 201
5. **Novels** (amazon.com/author/msbarnes)
   Folie¿ (a creepy, psychological thriller)
   Meet Frank King (psychological thriller)

The Emerald Tablet
101

A modern, practical guide, plain and simple

by Matthew S. Barnes

DEDICATION

I'd like to dedicate this book, first and foremost, to all the seekers out there. For us, life is a limitless playground.

I'd also like to dedicate this book to those of you that are open-minded and tolerant of other viewpoints. Sometimes it is hard being a seeker- there are so many people out there that are intolerant and fearful of any ideas outside the ones that they themselves have become accustomed to. Nowhere is this more clearly demonstrated than in religion, with the one obvious exception being politics.

I have had the opportunity to study with quite a few people from quite a few different religions, as well as people from different denominations within the same religion.

I am always surprised at how adamantly each person from each religion and each denomination can be that their viewpoint, and their viewpoint alone, is the only one that is even remotely correct. Their name for God, for example, has to be the only correct name for God. Their methods of worship must be the only acceptable methods. Most religions adamantly and emphatically believe all other religions to be praying to a completely different God, and obviously the wrong one.

Allah and Yahweh, for example, cannot be the same deity. It cannot be that people the world over have searched for and found the same ultimate truth, simply giving IT a name unique to their own nationality, culture, language and understanding. It cannot be that we are all searching for the same thing, in our own ways.

The entire situation reminds me of a child who claims his or her dad to be capable of beating up all the other dads. It seems that even when we seek the eternal we cannot get past our own childish and egotistical need to win, our need to be the only one that is right.

Those that are adamant that they are correct, and the only ones that are correct, cannot seem to fathom that others believe just as deeply in their own religion, in their own denomination, in their own scriptural interpretations. It seems a concept completely beyond their ability to comprehend or assimilate.

Recently, I had a very good friend try to get me to attend her church. She had been trying to get me to attend her church for quite some time. On this occasion I made the comment that I am always so surprised at how divisive religion can be. That not only are most people absolutely certain that their religion, and only their religion, is correct, but also that their denomination, and only their denomination, is the only correct one. I told her I simply did not think this way. This person assured me, adamantly, that it was not this way with her church. She seemed offended that anyone could think that way.

I then mentioned that I had studied with Jehovah's Witnesses as well as Mormons. My friend became very stern and told me that neither of those religions were Christian, or even Biblical. I went on to mention other denominations and religions, and a few beliefs and interpretations from those religions. Each time, she sternly made it known that those beliefs, religions and denominations were not Biblical and were therefore obviously wrong. When I mentioned how divisive her beliefs seemed, she had no idea what I was talking about. She didn't feel that she was against other religions and denominations at all. In fact, she felt that she was being very tolerant and open-minded.

Religion is an odd thing, right up there with politics. It seems that these two subjects are capable of transforming plainly rational people into emotional, irrational and often hatefully intolerant beings. This friend I just mentioned is a very good person, but when she starts talking about other religions and denominations, her demeanor changes completely. She transforms in front of my eyes from a sweet, accepting and motherly-type figure into a stern, cold and intolerant taskmaster. It is as if she has been brainwashed, and the name of other religions and other denominations are the trigger words that have been implanted in her mind in order to send her into a pre-programmed hypnotic state of anger and intolerance. I've seen the same reaction, the same instantaneous switch in personality, play out in the mere mention of politics as well.

I have another friend that is a youth minister. He was proud of the fact that he was teaching his class about Islam. It made him feel open minded. I was impressed and very curious, especially since the denomination this person belongs to is very well known for its intolerance towards other denominations. Also, the only book I ever knew him to read was the Bible.

As my friend began to explain to me what he had learned, it became obvious that he had obtained his information from some very skewed sources. When I asked him where he had learned the teachings of Islam, he claimed it to be straight from the Koran. However, when I asked to see the book, he brought out a Christian interpretation of the Koran, written by a very denominational Christian who was known for his intolerant views.

The book basically claimed the Christian religion to be correct and infallible, so anywhere the Koran strayed from Christian teachings was proof of the falseness of the Koran. The book then goes on to point out the difference in Biblical and Koran teachings, proving the falseness of Islam as a religion.

My friend adamantly and emphatically believed he was learning true Islam from this book and saw no need to read the Koran on his own, without input from anyone else, or to talk to an actual Muslim. In fact, he seemed genuinely puzzled that I did not feel that he was really learning true Islam, but instead a skewed interpretation through the eyes of another religion. How would he feel, I asked, if a Muslim taught other Muslims about the Christian religion? How would he feel if Muslims learned the Bible through an Islamic explanation written by a staunchly religious Muslim that was intolerant of the Christian religion?

That would obviously be different and wrong, my friend responded. They would not be getting the true teachings of the Bible, for the teacher would obviously skew the teachings. But since he felt the Bible to be the absolutely correct and infallible Word of God, but the Koran was not, he honestly felt it was ok for Christians to teach Islam to Christians in this manner; just not the other way around.

There is a very old parable that teaches that God created us all and put the truth into our hearts, uniting all of mankind. The Devil then came along and skewed that truth, twisting it into the different religions, thereby using God's own truth to divide mankind and create chaos and disunity among us. As I look around, I see this parable at work.

How many wars have been fought in the name of religion? How many people have died over differences in religious belief? How much division do we see just in America today due to religious intolerance?

Even now as I write this paragraph, there is a news headline on Yahoo citing American religious unrest. Evidently, a large group of the Christian population is upset because they feel they are being singled out and persecuted by US Laws that will not let them single out and persecute lesbians and gays. These people are literally claiming to be persecuted because they are not being allowed to persecute others.

We seem to want freedom for ourselves, but do not wish to grant it to others. We seem to want freedom of religion, but only as long as it is our religion we are being granted the freedom to practice. What we most want for ourselves we seem least likely to grant to others.

We seem comfortable with intolerant laws and religious practices, as long as those laws and religious practices are aimed at a group other than our own. America was founded by a population that fled Britain largely to gain the freedom to practice the religion of our choice, yet we are quickly becoming the intolerance that we once fled. We seem to be accepting of such behavior though, as long as we are the intolerant ones, and the intolerance is aimed at others.

The irony of the parable mentioned above is that if it is correct, then it is the most religious among us, the most divisive among us, that are most serving the Devil's desires of division, disunity, intolerance and chaos. Those that claim most to serve God may in fact be doing the exact opposite.

I believe that we are all, every single one of us, in the same boat. I believe that we all have the same questions and fears and insecurities. Black, white, yellow, brown; every person of every race, every land, every creed, every sex, every color- we all have the same fears, desires and insecurities. We want to be loved. We don't want to be alone. We want to have enough money or food or shelter to survive and to provide for those that we love. We all want to know why we are here. Is there a purpose? Is there anything after this life? We are unified more than we are divided; we are more alike than we are different.

In every time period and in every land there have been those that have had an "awakening", or have had a near death experience. Those that have had these experiences have all emerged with a similar tale to tell- a tale of a life beyond this one, and a tale of a loving Intelligence beyond this world.

Some of these people have been unknown, while some have been very well known, like Jesus and Buddha and Muhammad. In either case, the experiences of these teachers from each time period and geographical location are what eventually evolved into the different religions that we now know.

At the center, at the core, of each one of these teachings is this one unified belief- that life goes on, and that there is some sort of loving Intelligence behind it all. The flavor of each teaching may seem a little different, as each comes from a different culture during a different period of time, but it is all the same core belief. This fundamental belief is the key, the uniting factor of all regions, and the starting point for all spiritual practices.

Where we as a people seem to get caught up is in the extraneous commentary that has been added to each religion. In Islam, women are to cover their heads. In Judaism, you are not to eat pig. In Christianity, women cannot hold a position in the clergy. These are all examples of rules and regulations that have been added to the core teachings of the founders over the years, usually not by the founders themselves.

Most religious documents were written many years, at least fifty or so, after the death of the founder. What seems evident is that the founders are responsible for the core teachings as mentioned above, but the added commentary comes from the men that followed, men that had not awakened or seen beyond this world. To that point, the teachings of each religion often took on a life of their own after the passing of their founder, very often not even resembling the original focus of their founders.

Many of our religions even seem to stand for exactly the opposite of what their founders taught.

The core teachings of most religions, as previously mentioned, revolve around the belief in a life after the death of our bodies, a Universal Intelligence behind all that exists, and an earthly goal to live in a just, compassionate and generous manner. It seems that the previously mentioned parable of the Devil twisting God's love into religion in order to divide man plays out not only in the realm of overall organized religion, but also within each individual religion as well. Over and over, the loving teachings as expressed by most of our religious founders seem to have been transformed by later adherents and the masses back down into hateful and divisive bureaucracies that are obsessed with money and power. Individual egotistical intolerances have also found their way into the mainstream teachings of most religions. What is meant to be uplifting, uniting and divine is instead continually drawing us as a society back down into the lowest common denominator of division and angst. It is as if God keeps trying, IT keeps sending messengers, but as per the parable, the Devil keeps winning.

The core focus of Jesus' teachings was in helping the poor and healing the sick, yet modern Christianity seems to have all but abandoned this focus. Instead, modern Christians seem to be beyond obsessed with arguing scripture, wagging their fingers at other religions and denominations, treating God as a wish-granting Genie, and dedicatedly promoting ideas that are anti-poor, anti-gay, anti-environment, anti-intellectual, anti-immigration and anti-science. These practices seem to be in direct opposition to the way Jesus lived and taught.

When Muhammad of the Islamic religion was alive, he did much to elevate the status of women. We all know how that has changed.

During Muhammad's life, Muhammad also taught religious tolerance towards the Jews and the Christians. He felt that all three religions were of one lineage; it was just that the Christians and Jews were living from the old Word. Just as the Christians feel the Jews follow God's old Law, so too do the Muslims feel about the Christians. The Muslims feel Muhammad brought new teachings, and like the Jews before them, the Christians failed to update.

Still, Muhammad taught that this was no reason to hate or despise the Jews or Christians. They were still brothers, just followers of the older ways. Muhammad even allowed Muslims to marry Christians and Jews and went so far as to recommend having a Christian or Jewish spouse that had passed away buried in the manner of their particular religion. All this changed dramatically after Muhammad's death.

It seems that the religious ferment and fervor we so enjoy is of our own creation. The founders of the great religions did not seem to follow such beliefs or behavior, no matter how adamantly we add their names to our own beliefs and our own behaviors.

Religion is not supposed to be a system of intolerant beliefs, or an opportunity to brag of one's own virtue and correct scriptural interpretation. Instead, according to our founders, it is meant to be an exploration common to us all into the very nature of existence, and what lies beyond. It is meant to be a guidebook into living compassionately and rightly, helping those that are less fortunate.

The moral visions of our founding fathers have been overthrown and largely forgotten. I dedicate this short book to those of you with the guts to explore anyway, to those of you that are open-minded and tolerant, and to those of you who are truly trying to see the unity of life and make this world into a more compassionate and livable place.

Religion is one of the most powerful forces this world has

ever known, both for good and for bad. Let us try to make it for the better. Let us take the same ferment and fervor that so many use to exclude and to judge, and use it instead for the betterment of mankind.

CONTENTS

INTRODUCTION

The Emerald Tablet, also known as the Smaragdine Tablet, is an ancient artifact purportedly molded out of a single piece of green crystal. On the tablet is written fourteen cryptic sentences that are said to sum up the secret to Alchemy.

According to the legend surrounding The Emerald Tablet, a man named Balinas discovered the tablet in a vault below the statue of Hermes Trismegistus, an ancient Egyptian philosopher who is credited with being the author of the tablet. Inside the vault was an old corpse, possibly Hermes, on a golden throne. In the hands of the corpse was held the Emerald Tablet. There are other variations to this story, but this is the general gist of the tablet's legendary discovery.

There are now many different variations and interpretations of the writings on the Emerald Tablet. No two interpretations are identical and there seems to be no way to know for certain exactly how the original interpretation was worded. However, the basic meaning of the different writings seems to be about the same.

Alchemy is the ancient belief that, through chemical trans-formation, similar to the chemical transformations found in modern chemistry, one could turn a base element like lead or mercury into something much more precious, like gold. I believe that this Alchemical process is not meant to be taken literally, but is instead symbolic of the process and progression of a lower human consciousness into something much higher and more expansive. Instead of Alchemy representing a literal transformation of a base metal like lead or mercury into gold, I believe it represents the transformation of a base human being, ignorant and full of ego, into something of a higher nature- a spiritually matured, knowledgeable, compassionate and enlightened human being.

In most spiritual traditions, there seems to be an outer teaching that is taught to the masses and a secret inner teaching that is reserved for the inner circle of students. The outer teachings tend to include the basics of that particular religion's beliefs as well as rules for being nice to each other, or at least decent. In Christianity, for example, the outer teachings include the Ten Commandments, the Golden Rule and other guidelines for proper behavior.

The inner teachings in all religions are said to be what was taught from teacher to student within the inner circle. These teachings tended to be closely guarded secrets. If they were written down, they were typically written in a code that only the members of the inner circle, or those that were ready for the teachings would be able to decipher. The inner teachings offered instruction that went far beyond the simple outer teachings as taught to the masses. These inner teachings were typically more advanced studies on the ultimate reality of life as opposed to the simple instructions on proper behavior as taught to those outside of the inner circle.

A simple example of the difference between the inner teachings and the outer teachings is the idea of jihad, as found in the Islamic religion. In general, jihad refers to a holy war that we are all meant to partake in, and for which there is great reward. Many Muslim adherents take this to mean a true physical war, complete with gruesome violence against all non-believers. But the inner teaching is that the jihad is actually a war within you- a war between what is good and right within you versus your inner darkness. Another way of expressing this idea is that the inner war is between your self-centered ego and your higher self.

This inner jihad is a war that we are all engaged in at all times. It is *the* war we are here to fight- not a war with other people, but a war within ourselves. It is our ultimate destiny to take on and eventually defeat the darkness within us. Once freed from this darkness we experience the nirvana or heaven promised to us in the many different religions- a reward so far beyond anything we can comprehend that no words could adequately describe its allure. This, along with instruction on how to go about this war, is the inner teaching on jihad.

I believe the fourteen cryptic sentences on the Emerald Tablet to be a code written in symbolic language that only an "initiate" or inner student of Hermetic philosophy would be able to understand. Writing these teachings in code was meant to protect the teachings from those that were not yet ready for such information. I believe the fourteen statements of the tablet, once understood, basically sums up the inner teachings of the ancient Egyptian philosophy of Hermes Trismegistus, which have been passed down from teacher to student over the centuries. I am not alone in this view.

The name Hermes Trismegistus basically means Hermes "the thrice-great". This was the Egyptian way of expressing just how highly they thought of this man and his teachings. He and his teachings were so regarded that the Egyptians equated Hermes with their god Thoth and the Greeks equated him with their god Mercury.

Hermes had been a life-long student of both science and religion. He felt both subjects to be essentially the same pursuit- the pursuit of knowledge. Religion was the study of God, while science was the study of what God had created. Ultimately, both studies pointed to the same truth- the presence of an underlying Intelligence behind the workings of this world. This world is not randomly put together, and for Hermes this indicated an Intelligence of some kind.

Religions tend to personify this Intelligence. They like to give this Intelligence a face and a form and a name. They like to define this Intelligence, speak for this Intelligence and punish those who oppose their particular teachings on this Intelligence. Religion often breeds intolerance.

Scientists can be just as bad- the more they learn of this world the more they somehow seem to lose the mystery of it all. The more they think they can explain the less mysterious life seems to be for them. It is as if understanding the mechanisms behind a miracle somehow makes the miracle less miraculous or special. If, for example, a scientist can plot out and understand how an egg and a sperm come together to form an embryo, and how that embryo forms and grows, then somehow this knowledge diminishes their appreciation for the miracle of birth. Science often breeds arrogance.

These two studies, science and religion, are often at odds with each other. They both seem to feel that they operate on opposite ends of a spectrum, and each group feels that they alone represent the correct pursuit. For Hermes, this was not the case. He saw the two approaches as one-and-the same, simply two different angles of studying and searching for the Intelligence behind the workings of this world.

Unlike many of our modern religions, Hermes claimed that the Intelligence that we call God could not truly be named, for IT was beyond names. IT could not be drawn, for IT was beyond form. IT could not even be understood; for IT was beyond anything we could yet comprehend as humans. Speaking for IT was something none of us had the understanding to do. Taking another's word as the gospel truth was just as erroneous- this Intelligence is something each one of us must experience in order to have even the slightest understanding of ITs nature.

Unlike many scientists, Hermes saw in the pursuit of scientific knowledge the proof of this Intelligence's hand in every single aspect of life. Only chaos was an accident. In life there was order, and order demanded intelligence. From the rhythm of the seasons to the routine and predictable routes of celestial objects there was order. From the cohesion of atomic particles to the miracle of birth and the life cycle of all living things, Hermes saw order and therefore intelligence. Science was proof.

The more Hermes learned about the impeccable order of the universe, the more he saw within it the hand of order and design. The more he understood about the workings of this world, the more miraculous it became for him- not less, as is so often the case with so many scientists.

Eventually the knowledge and understanding Hermes obtained over many years of study and deep contemplation culminated in a vision he had of the Intelligence of this world. From that point forward he claimed to be "reborn", "born again", "enlightened", "awake". He had transcended the limits of his mind and had come to understand the ultimate truth of this world. He claimed that the experience he had was transformational in a way that we human beings could not yet comprehend. As such, he went about trying to teach others the knowledge that he believed would lead to the same vision and subsequent awakening, as he was so lucky to have experienced.

Hermes had found, through direct experience, "The Soul of the World". He had witnessed creation and was taught the meaning of Life. The Egyptians believed this knowledge transformed him into a god among men, and that with the same knowledge and effort you could do the same.

The overall goal of the ancient Egyptian teachings of Hermes, as summed up in the Emerald Tablet, was to enlighten each individual student with the specific knowledge that would eventually and ultimately lead to a direct experience with the Truth of this world. This direct experience is the core goal of Hermes' philosophy.

Each person must have their own direct experience with "The Soul of the World" to even come close to understanding IT. There is no relying on what another person has said or claimed. Reading scriptures and hearing other people contemplate God and Heaven are all second hand experiences that are no substitute for direct knowledge. Taking another's word for the Divine nature of this world falls far short of the magnificence of the actual experience. Actual experience is proof beyond a doubt, whereas faith alone is simply taking the word of another- it is secondhand belief.

After having studied the other writings of Hermetic philosophy for many years, I believe it is possible to understand and decipher the code of the Emerald Tablet, which is what I am trying to do in this short book.

Hermes' teachings are recorded mostly in a work called *The Hermetica*. He is also credited with writing *The Emerald Tablet*. In the end, scholars believe both works were probably written not by Hermes but by several other authors who were familiar with Hermes' teachings.

The Kybalion is another possible Heremetic work that represents core Heremetic teachings. However, this work was published by a group called the "Three Initiates" in 1912, long after the time of Hermes.

The Three Initiates claim that *The Kybalion* represents the inner teachings of Hermes that had, until that point, only been passed down from teacher to student over thousands of years. The writers of *The Kybalion* also claim that there had been a book by the same name that was given only to inner students, called initiates, of the Hermetic teachings, and that the version of *The Kybalion* that they were publishing simply covered a few of the more simple yet core inner teachings.

There were many other works representing Hermes' philosophy that were evidently destroyed by intolerant religions many years ago.

To better understand why I interpreted *The Emerald Tablet* the way I did in this book, it would be helpful for you to also read my interpretation of *The Hermetica*, and maybe *The Kybalion*. These are short books, though longer than this one, that go into more detail on the vision of Hermes and the overall Heremetic philosophy. I named my books *The Hermetica 101* and *The Kybalion 101*.

Although largely unknown in the West today, it cannot be overemphasized how influential the ancient Egyptian philosophy espoused by Hermes has been, mostly un-credited, on our modern discoveries, our modern thought system and even our modern religions.

Hermes taught that in his vision, he saw directly that at least part of the purpose of human life was to create and explore, as the Intelligence that created this world and us also creates and explores. Creating and exploring is what we like to do, and what we are meant to do. Science and God are not at odds. Science is simply the study of what God created. When one does not agree with the other, it is due to our limited understanding. Exploring this world through observation, scientific study and the arts are all joyful for us as human beings because it is at our core. We were made in the image of that which created us, and as IT finds joy in exploration and creation, so do we.

This teaching is in direct and stark contrast with many religious views that science and religion are at odds, and that all one needs to know is in the Bible of their religion. Searching and exploring outside of this holy book is often considered sacrilege. This is especially true of the early Christian and Islamic religions that banned the Hermetic teachings and burned their books.

The Hermetic belief that we are here to create and explore was the impetus behind countless modern discoveries and many scientists and great thinkers of the past have credited Hermes with being the foundation of their belief system. In fact, throughout history, when the teachings of Hermes were allowed, society flourished, as happened in the Renaissance, where spiritual and scientific curiosity was encouraged.

Heremetic philosophy was considered the driving force behind the Renaissance or "Rebirth", where free thought, creativity and exploration were encouraged. The famous Library of Alexandria is a prime example of the open-minded exploration of this time. This library contained countless books from countless foreign nations espousing theories and belief systems that were fervently and openly explored and debated. During this time, society flourished.

The intolerant early Christian Church disagreed with this philosophy, believing that all that we should be exposed to would be found in the Bible. As a result, the books were burned, the Library of Alexandria was destroyed, and those working the library were tortured and put to death. Dark times ensued.

The Emerald Table is reported to have been buried around 400AD to protect it from such religious zealots who wanted to destroy it.

Ironically, many of the teachings found in our modern religions can be traced back to the ancient Egyptian views of Hermes. Modern religions have, in very many cases, adopted the teachings and philosophies that Hermes espoused, but inserted their own heroes and their own specific vocabulary representing their teachings into their individual religions. This fact is mostly unknown to the proponents of these modern religions.

According to Heremetic teachings, we as humans grow in consciousness and compassion over time. We start out our journey as humans full of ego and individual concern. Over time, and possibly over many lifetimes, we eventually ripen and mature into a being of higher nature. This is Alchemy. Once we ripen and mature to a certain point, it is time to move on to the next realm after death.

By this philosophy, there is no good or bad, there is only mature and "not-yet-mature". Those of us who seem good have simply matured more. Those of us who seem bad are simply not yet ripened. We all make this journey, so there is no room for judgment or feeling superior. Those who are fairly advanced now were once just as ignorant and angry and self-centered as those who are not as of yet at this heightened level.

Over time, our understanding, our consciousness and our compassion expands beyond our individual self and individual concerns. We are all on this journey. We all eventually make this trip. The ultimate goal of the Hermetic teachings is to speed up this evolution so that we may pass on to the next realm sooner. Additionally, expanding your consciousness may also lead to a direct experience with the "Soul of the World" in this lifetime, which would transform your life here and now- taking you to a life beyond suffering and the human concerns that now drive you to anger and fear. If you knew that you were divine and would go on after death, what could possibly shake your peace of mind? If you knew without a doubt that you were safe, what could possible make you fret? Money? Illness? Social status? These things are as nothing once you see the truth, says Hermes. What now could possibly upset you?

With this knowledge, you become the Master of your own life, not the servant. You become as if a god among men. This is the ultimate goal of *The Emerald Tablet, The Hermetica* and *The Kybalion.*

A TRADITIONAL INTERPRETATION

The following represents a very typical interpretation of the Emerald Tablet, which is why I chose it. If you wish to be exposed to other interpretations, see the References at the end of this book.

1. Truth, most certain, beyond doubt
2. As above so below, as within so without, in order for the miracles of the one thing to be performed
3. As all things have been and arose from the one, so all things have their birth from this one thing by transformation
4. The sun is its father, the moon is its mother, the wind has carried it in its belly, the earth is its home
5. Its force of power is entire if it be converted into earth
6. Separate the earth from the fire, the subtle from the gross, with great care and diligence
7. It rises from the earth to heaven and then falls back again to the earth, receiving the power of both heaven and earth
8. By this means you will rule the world
9. And all darkness and ignorance will leave you
10. Its power is above all power, for it creates and destroys every single thing, and penetrates every thing as well, subtle and solid alike
11. By this means was the world founded

12. And hence come the miraculous adaptations
13. I am called Hermes Trismegistus, having understood the three parts of the philosophy of the world
14. I am done explaining the solar work

MY INTERPRETATION

In this chapter, I break down the traditional interpretation included in chapter one, explaining each statement line by line.

Remember that this is my interpretation of the Emerald Tablet based on my understanding of the Hermetic philosophy. To better understand my interpretation, and any interpretation really, it is helpful to have some background knowledge of the other Hermetic writings. My two other books on this ancient Egyptian philosophy, *The Hermetica 101* and *The Kybalion 101* are available if you need or want them.

There are many other viewpoints and interpretations of *The Emerald Tablet*, ranging from much more esoteric to much more scholarly. If you are interested in other viewpoints and interpretations, there are countless other books and even Internet sites that you can browse. I have listed my favorite web page for this work in the Reference section at the end of this book.

As I have done in my other works, I do not try to give a scholarly, historically accurate interpretation of these writings. Instead, what I am after is the big picture. I am after the ultimate meaning. I am attempting to capture the essence of what the Emerald Tablet is trying to say, as I understand it. If I do not seem interested in following a traditional interpretation that may be more scholarly or historically accurate, it is because I truly am not interested in that kind of interpretation. I simply want to put forth what I think the writing means, in the simplest, most modern and understandable concepts I can come up with.

"Seek not to walk in the footsteps of the wise, seek what they sought." – Basho

1 - Truth, most certain, beyond doubt

I, Hermes Trismegistus
Will now tell you
The Truth of this World

This Truth
I am about to reveal to you
Does not come
From idle speculation

Nor is it simply
My opinion
Or some fanciful theory
I heard from another,
Or read in a book
Or sacred scripture

No,
The Truth I now reveal to you
Comes from direct experience,
From direct knowledge-
As such,
It is beyond
The idle debate
Of the masses

What follows
Is simply and utterly
Undeniably and absolutely
The ultimate Truth
Of this World

For I have seen IT

2 - *As above so below, as within so without, in order for the miracles of the one thing to be performed*

Within and beyond this world
Is an Intelligence
That cannot yet be fathomed,
Or even imagined

I have seen this Intelligence
And though many
Would call IT God,
There are no words
For what IT truly is,
For IT is beyond conception,
And no name
Or description
Could do IT justice

IT is formless
Yet has form

IT has no substance
Yet IT does

IT seems as if
IT is a great Light
Of Awareness
Or Consciousness
That is completely beyond
Anything that can even be imagined-
There is nothing in this world
To compare IT to

This Intelligence

Is both within you
And all around you,
Both in this world
And in the next

IT exists in a realm
Just beyond
The one that we now know,
Yet ITs Essence
And Intelligence
Permeates this world as well,
Creating and animating
All that is

Behind the existence
Of all that you know
And all that you do not know
Is this One Thing,
This Light,
This Consciousness,
This Awareness,
This Intelligence

There is but One Substance
In all of existence,
And *This* is IT

It is for this reason
That I say
That What lies beyond this world
Is the same
As That which lies within this world,
And that What lies within you
Is the same
As that which surrounds you-
It is all the same base Substance,

It is all the Light,
Made manifest
In a multitude
Of different forms

The world is Divine
And an absolute miracle
If you could but see

The miracle continues
Into the construct
Of the material world,
As I witnessed the whole
To be no different
Than the part

The world is constructed
Of a holographic unity
That repeats itself
In an endlessly infinite continuum
On grander and lesser scales
In every direction
Forever

That which exists
On the greater scale
Is mirrored
By that which exists
On the smaller scale

That which exists
At the macroscopic level
Is mirrored
By that which exists
At the microscopic level
Let me explain…

The atom
Is the most basic
And most fundamental
Building block of Life

The atoms
That we are familiar with
Are infinite
And clump together
To create the world we know-
Every single structure,
Every single form

Our atoms
Ultimately come together
To form a larger atom-
The solar system,
Whose nucleus is the sun
And whose electrons
Are the planets
Orbiting endlessly about

Our solar system
Is but one atom
Out of an infinite number of atoms
That also come together
Creating an even larger Universe,
Or realm,
Or dimension,
Whose scale
Is beyond comprehension

In the opposite direction
We have within each of our atoms
Another Universe,
Or realm,

Or dimension,
Made up of smaller atoms,
Likewise infinite in number,
Beyond our ability to sense
Or fathom

Within each of those atoms
Is yet another Universe,
Or dimension,
Or realm,
Made up of even smaller atoms,
Likewise infinite in number,
Likewise beyond our ability to sense
Or even fathom

At each level
Is there a world or dimension
Vibrating at a frequency
And existing on a scale
That we cannot detect
Or hardly imagine

Do you yet see the miracle?
Do you yet see
The ladder of life,
Repeated endlessly,
In ever larger
And ever smaller units,
Expanding into eternity
In either direction forever,
Creating worlds and dimensions
Without end?

All the worlds are separate,
Yet in reality
All are One continuous Unity,

All being made
Out of this One Thing,
This One Substance,
This One Intelligence
That is beyond names
And beyond forms,
Yet is the root of all names,
And the root of all forms

What IT is
Is the Soul of the World

As is the next world
So is this world,
As is the larger world
So is the smaller world,
As is the inner world,
So is the outer world

All is separate,
Yet somehow,
At the same time,
All is One,
And the same

Such is the construct
Of this great,
Mysterious and magical world
Whose origin is an Intelligence
Beyond that of which
We can scarcely conceive

3 - As all things have been and arose from the one, so all things have their birth from this one thing by transformation

In the timeless beginning
There was only the One,
And IT seemed to me
As if it were
But a great Light
Of pure Consciousness,
As if Consciousness
Was a substance, and tangible-
And somehow
It was

The Light was an Intelligence,
An Energy
Beyond existence
And beyond my ability
To comprehend

This Energy
Was all that existed,
There was nothing else
But this Energy,
This Intelligence,
This Awareness-
IT was all that was
And IT was whole
And complete
In and of ITself

From this Intelligence,
From this One Thing
I saw emerge a Second-

A darker mass,
Heavier in substance,
Vibrating at a lower frequency

This Second
Was the world of matter,
And It was birthed
From the body
Of the Light
In one great explosion
Of Light and Energy
And Matter

This darkness
Was separate from the Light
Yet somehow
Still the Light,
For It had come
From the Light

The One
From whence the Second came
Was neither male
Nor female,
But the dark Second
Split into two-
A male and a female part,
A positive and a negative pole,
The yang and the yin,
The proton and the electron,
The alpha particle and the omega particle,
Representing the extreme range
From the most positively charged
And therefore most masculine particle
To the most negatively charged
And therefore most feminine particle

From this split
Came the union and repulsion
Of the male and the female energies and forms
Causing the Universe to divide and multiply
And to reproduced unendingly

From this process
Were all other things birthed
In this world

From the One
Came the Two

From the Two
Came the rest

Therefore the One,
In essence,
Created this world
By *becoming*
This world
And everything within it

There is but One Base Substance
That exists,
And this One
Has been *transformed*
Into the multitude of different forms
That we see around us

4 - *The sun is its father, the moon is its mother, the wind has carried it in its belly, the earth is its home*

In the timeless beginning
There was only the One

From the One
Came the Two-
A male and a female part,
A positive and a negative pole,
The yang and the yin,
The proton and the electron,
The alpha particle and the omega particle,
Representing the extreme range
From the most positively charged
And therefore most masculine particle
To the most negatively charged
And therefore most feminine particle

From this split
Came the union and repulsion
Of the male and the female energies and forms
Causing the Universe to divide and multiply
And to reproduced unendingly

The constant attraction and repulsion
Between the male and the female energies,
Between the positive and the negative charges
Generated a Life Force
That began to animate the Universe
(And still does)

IT is this Life Force
That enlivens our bodies,

Giving us Life
Every part, every cell and tissue and organ

As a battery
With its positive and negative poles
Produces energy
So too does this Great Battery
Produce Energy-
The Energy of Life,
The Life Force
That runs this World
And everything within it

The swirl of the negative electrons
Around the nucleus of an atom
Is the basic battery of Life
Producing Energy unending

The same holds true with the larger atoms-
The solar systems
With their nuclear suns
And the planets whirling around them

The same holds true as well
With atoms
On the smaller scales of existence,
As has already been mentioned

Future generations
Will call this Life Force,
This Energy,
Many things-
Ki and Qi
Prana and Mana
But like the Great Intelligence

That created the Generator
There are no words
That approach what this Energy
Really is,
What IT means or what IT does

Some even call It
The Holy Spirit
As this Energy
Is but the reunion
Of the One
That had become Two,
But through the interaction
Of the Two
Has once again
Became One

Since the interaction of the two charges
Is what gives birth
To this Energy of Life,
The positive particle
Can be considered as Its father
And the negative particle
Can be considered as Its mother

The Holy Spirit is an Energy,
Subtle, like the wind,
Moving in and out
Of all that is,
Animating whatever it touches
With Life and Light
And Awareness

Its home
And ultimate goal
Is within the forms

Of matter,
For that is where
It resides

5 - *Its force of power is entire if it be converted into earth*

The ultimate goal
And entire purpose
Of the Life Force or Holy Spirit
Is to inhabit and animate
The world of form

Were it not for the Life Force,
Matter would be dead and lifeless,
Without consciousness,
Without awareness-
Empty, void

Matter becomes alive
And aware
Only when animated
By this Energy,
Whatever It is

This occurrence,
This animation of matter with Life,
Is the entire purpose of creation

With this occupation
Of the Holy Spirit
Within the confines of matter
Is the final step of Creation
Ultimately achieved

6 - *Separate the earth from the fire, the subtle from the gross, with great care and diligence*

Matter,
Which is gross and heavy and coarse,
Is represented by Earth

Spirit,
Which is subtle and light and fine,
Is represented by Fire

As is the world around you
So too is your being-
Like the world at large,
Your form is made of Earth (matter)
But you are enlivened and animated
By Fire (Spirit)

The illness
Of the masses
Is that they believe
They are the body
That they inhabit,
Prone to illness
And decay and decline
And eventually death

They believe their body
To be the entirety
Of who and what they are,
And think they are ultimately
Destined to oblivion,
Along with the body
The truth
Is that we *have* a body,

But are not that body-
What we are
Is the Consciousness (fire)
Within that body (earth),
Infinite and immortal

Don't take my words
Or anyone else's words
As truth,
You must see this Truth
For yourself-
This is a necessity

The path is long and hard-
It takes years of learning
And study
And diligent observation-
Yet is worthwhile
In a way
I could never explain,
For the Secret within
Is a Treasure
Far beyond any treasure
This world
Could ever hope to offer

Within your body (earth)
And behind the thoughts
That fly randomly
Across the screen of your Mind
Is the Watcher within (fire)-
An Awareness,
A Consciousness,
An Energy, A Mind
That can never be destroyed,
For Energy

Is indestructible

See the distinction,
See the separation,
And from that point on
You are forever free

As often as possible-
Watch all that happens
Around you and within you
From that Still Place within...

As your body moves
And as your thoughts rise and fall
And the world and all its dramas and dreams
Seem to spin chaotically around you,
Stay calm in the Center
Within your core
And simply watch

There is nothing else
For you to do,
There is only something
For you to see

Watch your body move,
And watch your thoughts and emotions
As they rise and fall
And fade away

What is it within you
That is doing the watching,
Unattached to the dramas of this world?

What is it within you
That is doing the watching,

Safe and unharmed,
And untouched by this world?

It is the Watcher within,
It is you, the real you,
That is what It is-
You are the Watcher within,
Immortal and free

Explore with your Mind-
Can anything contain It?
Is it bound by time or space?
Can you not think of a place
And be there in an instant
In your Mind's Eye?
Can you not travel in time
Or explore the stars
And create worlds of your own
Within your Mind?

The Mind is eternal and free,
Unlimited,
Unbound

This Mind
Is who and what you are,
Not the body
That your Consciousness inhabits,
And not the thoughts
That you cannot control

Observe!
Contemplate these things
Well and often
And gradually
The Truth will build up

Within your understanding

Eventually
Your understanding
Will expand to the point
That it will overflow its borders
And the Truth will explode within you
Like a great Light
Illuminating all of Creation-
The world will open up
And unroll at your feet
And you will see,
And you will know
For a certainty

If you knew for sure
That you were not your body (earth),
Limited and mortal,
But instead
The Consciousness within (fire)-
Unlimited and Immortal-
What could then
Bother you in the least?

Illness?
Disease?
Poverty?
Low social status?

These things are as nothing
Compared to the Secret
That you now hold
Within

Awaken
And you will be

As if born again
Into a world
Free of suffering

You will see the separation
Of the body (earth) and the spirit (fire)

You will be able
To enjoy this world
And create and explore
Without a care in the world

I know these things
For a certainty,
For I awoke
And am now free,
Completely free-
And you can be
As well

7 - *It rises from the earth to heaven and then falls back again to the earth, receiving the power of both heaven and earth*

When I awakened
It was as if my Mind,
The Consciousness within Me,
Separated
From the body
I once thought
To be my entirety
And soared upward,
Or beyond,
Or within

It was as if
My understanding had expanded
To the breaking point,
And the borders
That had once contained It
Were overwhelmed
And overcome

Once free
My Consciousness burst forth
And expanded
In all directions forever-
There were no barriers left
To hold It in

Before my Mind's Eye
Opened a world and a truth
I could have never imagined
Had I lived
A million years,

And I experienced Myself-
My true Self
In My entirety,
As well as a Great Light
Of pure Consciousness
That emanated
From the Center of existence
Out into all that is
Was, or will be

I was overcome,
Filled to the Core
With Light
And Peace
And Love
And Knowledge

When my Consciousness
Returned to my body
It was as if
I were now two
Instead of the one,
For though I had a body
I now knew
That I and my body
Were not one and the same

I was the Consciousness,
The eternal Awareness,
Stubbornly inhabiting this body
And this world,
For a time

The paradox
Was that I had become
What I had always been

But never realized

I now live in this world
And enjoy its pleasures,
Unattached
Unafraid

What in the name
Of all that is Holy
Could I ever
Have to fear?
What could ever
Shake my peace
In the least?
For I am eternal,
Immortal and free

I am neither bound
By this world of matter
And time,
Nor tied to the decline and decay
And death
Of this body

I now possess
The power of both worlds,
Of Heaven and earth-
For I have the knowledge
Of my true identity
And also have the earthly realm
In which to create
And to explore
And to enjoy

It is said
That humans on earth

Are above
Even the gods in Heaven,
Who envy man,
For the gods
Have only
The immortal form,
While man possesses
The same immortal form
But also the earthly form
With which to enjoy
As well

I may still be in this world
But I am no longer of it-
And this I know
For a certainty

This world
Is not the extent of me,
Nor is this body,
And death
Is but the beginning

8 - *By this means you will rule the world*

The mass of humankind
Are not the kings and queens
Of their own castles,
But paupers and puppets instead

They do not rule
Their own lives
But tend to be ruled
By the world around them

They are dragged along
This way and that
By their wants and needs and desires
And the dramas and storms of life
Whirling about

Things go well
And they tend to be happy

Things go badly
And they tend to be sad

When they get what they want
They tend to be happy

When they don't get what they want
They tend to be sad

Completely out of their own hands
Is their peace of mind,
Their contentment,
Their happiness
Even when things do go their way,

The ultimate fear
Of decline and decay
And death
Steps in
And sits at the back of their mind
Gnawing away
At any short-lived happiness
Or peace
They may have been lucky enough
To obtain

Awaken
And the Truth of this world
Will open up before you
And all of this will change,
Forever

You will no longer fear death
As the masses do,
Or poverty
Or illness

Though the storms of life
May toss and roar
And throw you about,
And they *will*-
They will no longer
Hold any sway
Over the peace
In your mind and heart

Death can no longer touch you,
Nor can poverty
Or illness
Or decay
Whatever comes your way

You will be able
To enjoy,
Whatever goes away
Simply goes

You need nothing,
So nothing
Has any power over you-
None whatsoever

Then,
And only then
Can you enjoy everything

You will then have become
The king or queen
Of your castle,
And can drift happily
Through this life
Without a care in the world

You will have become
The ruler
Of your world-
You will have become
As if a god
Among men...

9 - *And all darkness and ignorance will leave you*

When that Light
Illuminates your Being
All darkness recedes,
For darkness is not equal
To the Light,
But merely the absence of IT

What is the darkness?
The darkness is ignorance-
The only real evil
In this world

Darkness, ignorance
Is but a lack of knowledge-
It breeds feelings
Of separation and fear,
Racism and sexism,
Patriotism and creedism,
Elitism and partisanism
Egotism and selfish concerns

This leads to envy and anger
And hatred
And violence
And suffering

But the Truth
Clears away the darkness
And fills us with a Knowledge
That erases all divisions-
The lines
That so seemed to separate us all
Melt into nothingness

The Truth
Fills us with a compassion
And an understanding
And an empathy
And a feeling of kinship
For all living things
Beyond that of which
You can now scarcely imagine,
For we do so love our divisions,
Do we not?
And the dramas
That they breed

Once Illuminated
You will see only eternity,
Only infinity,
Immortality,
Unity

Until then
You will see
Only decline and decay and death
And the divisions
That seem to divide us all

10 - *Its power is above all power, for it creates and destroys every single thing, and penetrates every thing as well, subtle and solid alike*

You may think
That you understand power,
But as of yet
You know nothing

Aggression
May seem powerful

Anger
May seem powerful

Your size and your strength
And your stubborn opinions
May seem
To give you power

You may think
That you are powerful
Because you have money
Or possessions
Or status,
Or because you have sway
Over other people

But these things are as nothing
Compared to the Power
That animates
The living world
The Power
Of which I speak
Spins galaxies,

Holds the stars in place,
And rotates the earth
On its axis

All that is
All that was
And all that will be
Was created
By this Power,
Whatever IT is

And all that is
All that was
And all that will be
Will be torn down
By the same Power
In time

Nothing escapes ITs grasp-
Not the smallest object in the world,
Nor the largest,
Not the hardest object in the world,
Nor the softest,
Not the toughest object in the world
Nor the weakest-
All are subject
To ITs power,
Including your body

No matter how wonderful
You may think you are,
You are as nothing
Next to this Power-
You are less
Than even a speck of dust
On a speck of dust

Your own individual power
Does not even register
Compared to the Power
Of which I speak

But the Great Power
Lies within you,
Untapped,
Unused

Awaken to ITs presence
And then you will know Power,
Real Power-
You will bear witness
To the greatest Force
Ever known

IT is already there,
Within you
And all around you-
You simply cannot see IT
Or use IT
As of yet

But you will,
Eventually,
And when you do
Not only will you master this world,
But you will surpass it,
For you will be filled
With all you will ever need
And more
Needing nothing
You will be free,
Completely free,
And unshackled

From the prison of insatiable cravings
That so rule the masses

That is freedom

That is Power

11 - *By this means was the world founded*

By this Power,
By this Intelligence
That is beyond comprehension,
And by this method
I have now disclosed to you,
Was this world founded
And everything within it created,
Structured,
Animated,
And filled with Life,
Awareness,
Intelligence,
Consciousness...

The One,
Timeless and formless,
Literally created this world
By becoming this world,
Transforming ITs own Essence
Into a myriad of forms
Through an Intelligent design

This One Thing,
This Intelligent Unity,
Split into a Second-
The world of matter,
The Universe,
The Son, if you will

The Son,
Unlike the Father,
Is dual-
Made of the positive

And the negative,
The alpha particle
And the omega particle

The One reformed
Back into this world
When the Two,
The positive and the negative,
Reunited through attraction

Thus was born the Holy Spirit,
Or Life Force, or Qi
That enlivens
And animates
This living world

The Father,
The Son,
And the Grandson
Are all,
In the end,
One and the same

By such was the world founded,
And formed,
And given Life

12 - *And hence come the miraculous adaptations*

By this method
Are all things of this world
And everything within it
Made,
Sustained,
And then reabsorbed

This world
And every square inch of it
Is a miracle-
Alive,
And filled with Intelligence,
Consciousness,
Awareness

There is nothing
That is created
Or that exists
That is not a miracle,
Made directly
Out of and by this One Thing,
And run by the same

The method
I have now released to you
Is ongoing-
It is played out
In every single second
Of every single minute
Of every single hour
Of every single day
Even now
As you read these words,

New life is forming
Out of The One Thing
And being imbued
With Essence
And Intelligence
And Awareness

Even now
As you read these words,
Old life is being broken down,
And reabsorbed
And redistributed

You have a body
And exist
And are aware
Right at this very moment,
At this exact instant,
Because of a living Force
Within you
That is even now regulating
And regenerating
And renewing your body,
Holding it together
And filling it with Life
And Consciousness
And Awareness

This process
Will go on
For every single second
Of your existence,
And for every single second
Of the existence
Of every living thing
In all of creation

13 - *I am called Hermes Trismegistus, having understood the three parts of the philosophy of the world*

My name is Hermes
And I have been given the title
Of Trismegistmus
Meaning Thrice Great
Because I have understood and revealed
The Trinity of Life-
The Trinity of the One

The Light of Consciousness
Is the elixir of Life-
The elixir of creation-
The One Thing
From which this world
And all within it
Have sprung

From the One
Came a Second-
The world of matter

The Second
Is separate from the One,
Yet somehow
Is still the One

From the two parts
Of the Second
(The male and the female,
The positive and the negative)
Came a Third-
The Holy Spirit

Or Life Force

The Holy Spirit
Is the reunion of the One
Within the world of matter

This Third
Is separate from the Second
And separate from the One,
Yet still
Somehow the One
As well

The One
Is the Father

The Second
Is the Son

And the Third
Is the Life Force
Or Holy Spirit

All three are separate,
Yet all three are One-
They are all
One unified whole

The Father,
The Son,
And the Holy Spirit

This is the Trinity
Or the Tri-Unity
Of Life-
The Trinity

Or the Tri-Unity
Of the One

14 - I am done explaining the solar work

This is my last writing
And my final attempt
At explaining
The Great Light of Consciousness
That exists beyond this realm
And creates and animates
This living world

The same Light,
The same Consciousness,
Exists within you as well

Study,
Observe,
Awaken...

MY EMERALD TABLET

The following fourteen statements represent my attempt at writing out my own Emerald Tablet.

I did not attempt to make the fourteen concepts cryptic or symbolic, as with the original, but instead tried to portray the *big picture* of what I believe the Tablet was trying to express.

1. What follows is simply and utterly, undeniably and absolutely the ultimate Truth of this World and What lies beyond. Through intense study and hard work I have been lucky enough to have experienced this Truth, and now wish to relay my experience to you...

2. Within and beyond this world is an Intelligence that cannot yet be fathomed, nor even imagined. This Intelligence is both in this world, and in the next; both within you, and all around you.

3. This Intelligence not only created this world, but *is* this world, for this world materialized out of ITs Essence. All that exists is merely transformations of this same Essential Energy into a myriad of forms.

4. The world of matter emerged from this Intelligence, this Energy, and then split into two opposing charges- the positive particle and the negative particle. From the attractions and repulsions of these two charges did this world reproduce into infinite forms. Additionally, the interaction of these two charges also reunited the two

separate halves back into the One Thing in the form of the Holy Spirit or Life Force that animates this living world. The interactions of the positive and the negative charges are as if *the battery of life.*

5. The Ultimate goal of this Life Force is to inhabit matter, imbuing it with life, consciousness, awareness, intelligence. This is the final step, and entire purpose, of creation. What is matter, without life?

6. With an open mind, intense study, an indomitable will and regular practices of deep contemplation you will be able to witness the separate existence of your body and the immortal Consciousness within it. This experience I call the awakening, or being born again.

7. The experience of awakening is as if the Consciousness within you suddenly breaks free of all constraints and you see that what you are is not the body you inhabit, which is doomed to decline, decay and death, but instead the Consciousness within that body, which is immortal and free.

8. With this awakening are you thus reborn into an existence beyond the reach of suffering and sorrow, where you experience the best of both worlds- you have the world of matter to explore and enjoy, yet with the knowledge of your immortality and the world beyond.

9. All ignorance will leave you and you will become free and wise, filled with a deep and enduring compassion for all living things.

10. You may think you have a concept of power, but the Power of which I speak is beyond any power you can now conceive. IT is beyond your ability to imagine, comprehend or fathom.

11. From this One Essential Substance was this world founded, animated and filled with life and light and intelligence.

12. All that exists is simply an ongoing transformation of this One Essential Substance into an infinite multitude of forms. This world is a miracle!

13. My name is Hermes, and I have been given the title of Trismegistus because I have experienced and told of the Trinity, the Triunal composition of this world, consisting of The Father (the One), the Son (the Universe, made from the One) and the Holy Spirit (the Life Force). All three are separate, yet all three are One and the same. All is the One Essential Substance.

14. This is my final work and my last attempt at trying to explain this Intelligence, this Light of Consciousness, and the path towards awakening to IT.

CONSIDER READING NEXT

Consider continuing the Egyptian Enlightenment Series:
Author page: amazon.com/author/matthewbarnes
- The Emerald Tablet 101: book 1.
- The Hermetica 101: book 2.
- The Kybalion 101: book 3.

Matthew's "Zennish Series" books can be read in any order, but Matthew meant for them to be read in the following order:
- Tao Te Ching 101
- Albert Einstein, Zen Master
- Tao Te Ching 201
- Jesus Christ, Zen Master
- Dr. Seuss, Zen Master

I may also be adding to the Hindu Enlightenment series. Check my author page for progress: amazon.com/author/matthewbarnes
- The Bhagavad Gita

Or consider one of MS Barnes' novels:
- Folie¿
- Meet Frank King

*Be warned that Matt's novels are not the same as his spiritual works, though they do dive heavily into the power of the mind.

REFERENCES

Over the years, I have read many different versions of *The Emerald Tablet*, mostly online interpretations. I have read scholarly approaches, extremely esoteric versions and more down-to-earth approaches.

I would have to say that my favorite online source would be found at http://www.sacred-texts.com/alc/emerald.htm. This web page offers around twelve different translations, citing the source of each translation. If you would like exposure to more information on The Emerald Tablet, I highly recommend this web page as a start. If you do your own web search you are likely to find *many* more translations as well.

As with my other works, what I am after in my translation of *The Emerald Tablet* is the "Big Picture". In a nutshell, and in modern terms and ideas, what is *The Emerald Tablet* really trying to say? This is what I tried to convey in this book- my understanding of what *The Emerald Tablet* is really all about.

As usual, I didn't follow each translation strictly, trying to say exactly what Hermes said, but instead tried to express what I felt he was trying to get across. Our times and Hermes' time are very different. I was attempting to give you the feeling and spirit of what I feel he meant, without being technical at all in preserving his original words.

AUTHOR BIO

Matthew Barnes is an avid learner who spent his early years in North Carolina. He was born in Greenville, NC and has lived in New Bern, Roanoke Rapids, Henderson (where he spent most of his childhood) and Raleigh, where he attended the University of North Carolina State. After obtaining degrees in Biochemistry and Chemistry, he attended Chiropractic School in Marietta, Georgia, where he graduated third in his class. Since that time, he has studied acupuncture and Chinese medicine, and settled down in rural Tennessee with his wife, 3 cats, 4 dogs, a crazy mother-in-law and a partridge in a pear tree. He has been in Tennessee for over 20 years now.

His main interests are learning, exploring, exercising and writing. Most of his works so far have been on spiritual-type themes, though he has also written a book on self-investing-another one of his hobbies.

To check the progress on his other works, go to:

http://www.amazon.com/Matthew-S.-Barnes/e/B00SDYKSZ2

Printed in Great Britain
by Amazon

57770387R00046